Roses & Thorns

To Martin

Maria Pia
♡

ROSES & THORNS

Open my heart and you will see, engraved inside of it, Italy.
Robert Browning

Maria Pia Genovesi Oliver

Cover image:

"Briar Roses"
a water-colour by Maria Pia Genovesi Oliver.

Printed by Amazon

I dedicate this book to the memory of my lovely Mamma who always had faith in me, to my family here and in Italy, and to all those who love me.

I thank my wonderful family with all my heart for their encouragement and their help in writing this book, and, of course, the Holy Spirit for His guidance. I especially thank Michael for his invaluable help in undertaking the compilation and publication of the book. Also, I am very grateful to our son Anthony for translating the original version into English.

Contents

My Childhood

My Adolescent Years

My Youth and Adult Life

Epilogue

Appendix - Paintings

Preface

I have tried to gather a collection of stories which look like snapshots taken by an invisible photographer, glimpses of my life over the years, but many memories have been left out to avoid boring the reader.

.

My Childhood

Villa Ida: Our Beautiful Villa

No, it was never ours, but Giovanna, Angelo, Valeria, Tonino and I believed it was and continued to do so until the terrible day when two characters came knocking, like the two 'bravi' sent to Don Abbondio in Alessandro Manzoni's famous novel 'The Betrothed'. Papa later told us they were the owners of the villa and they wanted to evict us. I felt my heart sink, and the memory can still upset me now, all these years later.

Reluctantly, we moved to a first-floor apartment in a building on the same street, but how could I forget our beloved home where I was born, where I played hide and seek with my brothers and sisters, and where we played with our friends next door? How could I forget the beautiful garden which wrapped around the villa and where every school-day morning at seven o'clock I revised Latin or History or Philosophy, or other subjects before heading off to school? What about the vegetable garden which Mamma had asked someone to turn over and sow, and where I happily went to pick beans for our dinner?

There was also an orchard, with plum trees, apple trees, and figs trees, but the most beautiful of all was a cherry tree which, when in season, would be loaded with cherries of a rich vermillion, and Mamma sent Valeria and me up with two baskets which were never quite filled, so juicy and large were those cherries.

Next to the orchard was the chicken coop where the hens went to sleep after roaming freely all day. How I liked going to collect the eggs, and how I loved the chicks which I, aged three, used to water every day to make them grow faster!

Maria Pia, one year old, with Angelo & Giovanna

Maria Pia at three years with Valeria, Giovanna & Angelo

2

The five Genovesi

Mamma & Papa

Et Tu Brute?

Behind the garden which surrounded the villa there was the orchard and, beside it, the vegetable garden. This area bordered the property of the elderly Berra sisters, Emma and Irene, with a fairly high wall. On the edge of their garden stood a plum tree with such beautiful and enticing fruits that one sun-drenched afternoon we decided to taste them. None of us gathered there was tall enough so we called Giovanna, the tallest of the five of us, and persuaded her to climb the wall, but what surprise was waiting for her on the other side ... Miss Irene's head popped up, yelling at the thieves! Poor Giovanna slid straight back down and we all collapsed with laughter. From that day on the incident was referred to as 'Et tu Brute', as you should understand that the Berra sisters and Giovanna enjoyed a friendly rapport and they would never have expected such a bold move from our sister. How could it have been possible, we wondered, that the Berra sisters knew our plan? We concluded that someone had spied on us.

The finger was pointed at two other ladies, the Arceci sisters, who lived behind our house and the Berra sisters' bungalow, giving them a grandstand view of everything happening under their noses. Furthermore, and I have no idea why, we never liked those sisters!

The Thieves

Papa lived in terror of thieves visiting the villa we lived in, especially after the house of our neighbour, lawyer Senaldi, was broken into. So, gripped by an irrational fear, every evening at a certain hour, he balanced a saucepan above every door, to the consternation of Mamma and us siblings. We were never ever visited by thieves – imagine the noise they would have made!

Jerico

Around the table in the dining room of our house, my place was next to Mamma, who sat at the head of the table while Papa sat at the other end, and my brothers and sisters filled in the remaining places.

When there was soup, which was not very thick, I would always fish out the pieces of celery, and arrange them around the rim of the bowl, as I had a great aversion to this vegetable.

Unfortunately, I never got away with this because all it took was a hard stare from Papa's handsome grey eyes to demolish my celery fortifications, which would return forlornly into the soup.

I still do not like pieces of cooked celery, which I always blend when I make soup or minestrone.

Single File

Papa had the habit of buying crates of seasonal fruit for the whole family of seven. He used to go to the wholesaler Milani and bargain for whole crates of grapes, apples and mandarins, which would then be delivered to the house.

Angelo, my eldest brother, had the great idea of an adventure, to the detriment of the supply of mandarins, as these were his favourite fruits. So, one evening Angelo instructed us to meet outside his bedroom, at the top of the stairs. As soon as we were sure our parents were fast asleep, we began descending the stairs in single file, Angelo first, 11 years old, followed by Tonino, five, Valeria, eight, me, just over nine, and Giovanna, 13, who could not stop laughing, while Angelo urged silence to avoid waking Papa!

Papa was a deep sleeper, yet that night he woke up; he must have heard something, and went into Angelo's room muttering to himself. Seeing a rounded shape in the bed, he went back to sleep, satisfied that the house was quiet. Angelo had planned ahead, and had placed some cushions under his blankets!

The Basket

In the blue sideboard in the dining room there was a wicker basket containing some bread rolls. The sideboard was always locked, apart from when it was opened to put the bread on the table. Bread was expensive, we were in the midst of a world war, the bread rolls were counted, there were seven of us and Mamma had to keep the sideboard locked to stop any of us helping ourselves to that precious bread.

Il Corrierino Dei Piccoli

How excited Valeria and I were when Il Corrierino dei piccoli arrived – this was the children's magazine Mamma used to buy for us every week. The rule was that we first had to help around the house, and then, as a reward, we could read it. We used to fight over it but since I wanted to really savour it, I remember that I used to wait before reading certain pages, such as the 'signor Bonaventura' story.

Dear Corrierino, how much joy you gave us!

Those Violets Were So Beautiful

Valeria, our friend Anna and I discovered that along the side of a long lane that lead to the Coerezza family villa some magnificent violets had bloomed under the pine trees – they were so inviting that we just could not leave them there. One beautiful afternoon we headed off towards that house and knelt down to pick as many violets as we could, the scent was intoxicating. I can still remember the joy we felt.

We made a return visit that Spring but someone had seen us, and one awful day we saw the owner coming down the lane holding a stick, and yelling at the top of his voice. What could we do but run back down the hill to our house?

Valeria and I soon reached our gate, and we headed up the steps without being seen, and hid under our parents' bed, but poor Anna, who was lame and could not run, incurred the wrath of signor Coerezza. We were lucky he did not come down to our house and complain to our parents.

How old were we? I do not remember exactly, but we must have been very young.

Ten Centimetres Below The Knee

Papa believed that girls should always wear skirts with hemlines ten centimetres below the knee. This made Valeria so cross, as she did not want to yield to his commands, and the family atmosphere would become heated.

I do not remember exactly how old we were, we were maybe just seven or eight, but Papa's rule continued into our teenage years.

What must he have made of the miniskirt era!

My Town Immersed In Silence And Darkness!

It was 1943, in the midst of the world war, and that evening a curfew had been declared. My town was immersed in darkness. In the candlelight of the kitchen, Mamma sat beside Aunt Lina as she read a letter from Uncle Arturo, her husband, who was a prisoner in Auschwitz. I have no idea how the letter reached Gallarate. He returned home after many years, but he was never the same again.

Papa And The First World War

Papa had already experienced the anxieties of a war. He would often tell us of when, aged 19, he was sent to fight the Austrians in Trentino-Alto Adige, at the command of an artillery detachment. He told us that one day, when the enemy lines were in sight, he ordered the men under his command to remain in the trenches, but the cook disobeyed him and was immediately hit. Papa ordered one of his men to go to the aid of the injured cook, but the soldier replied "You can go, Lieutenant". Papa did not report the soldier. He told us that Italian and British soldiers fought side by side and would exchange grappa and whisky. It was the Sassari Brigade that fought with the most honour, Papa was full of admiration for those Sardinians who won the Battle of Tre Monti, defeating the Austrians.

Now we were back in the middle of a World War, and Papa no doubt was worried about us all and how it would end for us.

Milan Burns

During the Second World War Milan, like other Italian cities, was bombed so intensely that its landscape was changed forever.

One night we were gathered together on the terrace of Villa Ida, where we lived, and our gazes were directed towards Milan, 40 kms away. The sky over the city was red with flame. I was just five years old, and I can still remember Mamma's heartfelt cry "They're bombing Milan!" I also remember that Tonino, just a few months old, was bundled up in a little coat. It was 1943.

Only recently, all these years later, did I discover, via the Internet, what happened in the city of my studies, when the bombs fell on everything, churches, houses and even hospitals.

A Cry In The Night

"Ingegnere! Ingegnere!" Someone was calling Papa from the street beyond our gate. It was our neighbour, the lawyer Senaldi, who was trying to alert us that an air raid of Allied bombers was coming.

I do not remember exactly which night it was, anyway this was not the first time, but the drill was to quickly get dressed, and run to the nearby hill, lie down on the grass under the stars, and wait for the planes to fly over. As children, we saw it as a game, but I am sure our parents had their hearts in their mouths.

Black Bread

During the war, Papa was appointed Mayor of Ferno, the small town where Mamma had been born. Since certain people believed that in our house we ate white bread as opposed to the regulation black bread, an official came to the house one day to see what colour bread we were eating. Mamma showed him the basket containing our bread: black bread!

It Is A Miracle We Survived

A scene I will never forget.

Tonino was standing on a chair while Valeria and I were transfixed by what had just happened: our celluloid doll had caught alight next to the fire, and was burning furiously. Just then Mamma knocked on the door, and I ran to open it.

Tonino would have been just two, Valeria six, and I seven; we were the three youngest, and Mamma had entrusted us to the live-in maid but, taking advantage of Mamma's absence, she was in her room upstairs doing gymnastics!

A German Cannon

One day a German cannon appeared on our street, like a bolt out of the blue! What on earth was a German cannon doing there? Our parents discovered the reason straight away: it was pointed at the church, on the same hill we sheltered behind, and which was also where the Aloisianum Institute, home of the seminary students, was located.

25 April 1945: Liberation Day

An unforgettable day in the memory of all Italians, especially the partisans who had never subjected themselves to the Nazi occupation and fascist regime.

I remember there was a great commotion everywhere, cars sounded their horns all over the city, trucks loaded with young people waving the Italian flag were chanting as people poured into the streets and squares to sing and dance, shouting "Long live freedom". Even we children rejoiced by clapping our little hands without understanding the full significance of the event. In Viale Noè, a few steps from home, parades of American jeeps and trucks passed by, and we little ones ran to see our liberators who handed us huge pieces of chocolate. What a joy!

25 April 1945

My Sweet Teacher

I remember how sweet my teacher, Mrs Rustioni, was, and I would have loved to have had her forever, but one awful day she lost her young life to illness. I recall the scene of her funeral as clearly as if it were yesterday. Her little boy standing before the coffin as it was lowered slowly into the grave, and the great sadness that enveloped me.

Another teacher came along after her; she was short, fat and wearing glasses, but I kept my sweet teacher Mrs Rustioni in my heart. She once told Mamma that I did not answer when she called out 'Genovesi' in the register, so Mamma told her "Try calling her Piuccia" and you will see that Pia answers.

Summer Camp

I do not have good memories of the 'Colonia' summer camp. Families in need would send their children to the various summer camps that local councils had set up near the sea, or in the mountains, so that children could enjoy clean air away from the cities. I especially remember the summer we ended up in Ossimo, a mountain village near Sondrio.

We were the three youngest, Tonino would have been not much older than four, Valeria seven and a half, and I would have been nine. I can still recall the scene when Tonino was made to stand up in front of all the children because he had wet the bed. I wanted to shout at the managers, but I stayed beside Tonino while Valeria showed her spirit by expressing her disapproval of our little brother's treatment in a loud voice.

For an afternoon 'merenda' snack they would give us half a slice of bread with a little moist sugar.

Very Shy

I was always shy and I still am. Colleagues of Papa often visited, and they were offered coffee. I do not know why Papa always asked me to carry the tray into the study, and I always imagine myself walking in and dropping the whole lot in front of the guests, so I tended to ask Mamma to do it instead, but sometimes I just ran upstairs and hid under the bed while Papa called "Pia, Pia".

The Three Doctors

When I was eight years old, I fell ill with pleurisy, and I had to stay in bed for a month in the dark because they thought it was contagious; only Mamma would come into the room. I remember that it was very hot, and I tried to find a strip of sheet my body had not been lying on, and moved from right to left, and then from left to right. I passed the time, for most of the day, reciting Ave Marias, one after another, until I fell asleep.

One day Papa appeared in my room with three men dressed in black; they looked like three crows, and they reminded me of the three doctors who visited Pinocchio in Carlo Collodi's classic story. What had happened was that Papa had gone against Mamma's wishes, and had called three separate doctors, and they had all arrived at the same time. I was too little to feel embarrassed, but I can imagine Mamma's consternation.

One month later I received my First Holy Communion along with Valeria, and the photograph that was taken shows me with a deathly pallor while Valeria beams brightly. I remember that I nearly fainted that day in Gallarate's large cathedral.

The Good Deeds

When I was nine years old, I recollect that I would help Mamma with some of the chores, such as cleaning the doors in spring, which I enjoyed doing, or washing clothes in the bathtub or at the laundry, which was behind our villa. Ironing had become one of my favourite jobs because I liked surprising Mamma when she had to go out, and I would leave piles of ironed clothes on the table for her to find on her return.

I can still see the floor which I allowed to dry in the sun shining in through the open window. But there was one thing I did not like, and which I still do not like doing: dusting!

Every time I thought I had done something good I would place a grain of rice on a saucer on my bedside table: they were my good deeds.

Mamma Unwell

I was around ten years old when Mamma fell gravely ill, and was taken to Sant'Antonio Abate Hospital in Gallarate. I was given the task of going to call Aunt Gina, Papa's sister, who lived in the town centre, to come and look after us. I took my bike and cycled with my heart in my mouth; at the junction I passed the ambulance taking Mamma to hospital, and I remember I cried out "My Mamma!"

Another sad memory was when one afternoon Papa was carried in because he had fallen from scaffolding while surveying a building. Papa was an engineer, and if the works were not carried out properly he would have them done again, something which made him rather unpopular among the local building companies.

My Adolescent Years

Difficult Years

The years following the end of the war were very hard for many families, including ours. Papa had lost everything, and therefore was not able to buy the beautiful villa we were renting, while many had transferred their savings to the safe haven of Switzerland.

Papa no longer had a car, the last one had been a Topolino, and he visited nearby towns to look for work on his Moschito, a bicycle with a small motor, but too often he came home disappointed. In winter he stuffed his jacket with newspaper to protect himself from the cold as he had nothing else.

I can still remember his face when he replied with a shake of his head to Mamma asking him how it had gone. Meanwhile she would encourage us children to support him, "Go and greet Papa," she would say sweetly.

Mamma often did not have the money to pay for the daily shopping, and we had to ask for credit. We had a separate credit book for the bakery, drug store, butcher and greengrocer. I can still see myself, 11 years old, in the Scampini bakery with the book listing our debt. She was very kind, and always gave me an olive oil bread roll to take home.

I felt great shame in these shops that gave us credit, but the greatest shame was when I went to the Levati bookshop to collect all the books for the first year of secondary school, and I had to tell them we would pay at the end of the month! Books for five children! Dear Mamma and Papa, so many sacrifices to allow us to study!

Secondary School

I do not have very happy memories of starting secondary school at the age of 11. The Maths teacher was a red-faced priest who would walk from one side of the class to the other, his hands inside his cassock, muttering something nobody could understand, and every now and then he would write something on the board. We lived in fear that he might aim a kick at us, so none of us dared ask for explanations. The result: nearly the entire class was made to repeat the exams in October. Mamma and Papa called a teacher for me from a nearby town, who was excellent, and I immediately understood everything, making peace with Mathematics.

I loved writing, and was happy when it was time for an essay test in Italian; my classmates asked me to help them with their work, but how could I write their essay for them? The day we received our marks I saw a great big four next to my name! Mamma tried to tell the teacher that I loved writing, but there was nothing to be done, and at the end of the school year I was told I had to retake Italian in October. The day after Mamma tried talking to her, that awful woman lifted up my paper in front of the whole class saying I had copied the essay, and that I had even sent my mother to make excuses. I felt so humiliated, and wanted to just disappear. Mamma had told the truth, that I loved writing.

Many years later I took comfort from the knowledge that the great writer Alessandro Manzoni, author of "The Betrothed" had failed the year in Italian!

That summer I was sent to have private Italian lessons with signora Losa, a jewel of a teacher, but after my first visit to her house she called Mamma to tell her I did not need any help with Italian!

Teacher Training

Once I had finished junior secondary school, I wished to enrol at the Istituto Magistrale di Gallarate, a secondary school channelling pupils towards a career in teaching, but Papa started to put pressure on me to choose a different school with the aim of becoming an architect, just because I loved drawing.

With the help of Mamma and her sweetness I talked Papa round, and enrolled at the Istituto Magistrale, where I was reunited with my dear friends from the primary and junior secondary school. The four years I spent studying there were happy, carefree times.

The Istituto Magistrale was run by the Canossian nuns, founded by Matilde di Canossa, and was exclusively for girls, while the Liceo Classico (secondary school focussing on Humanities) where Valeria was enrolled, was for both boys and girls.

The Latin Teacher

The Latin teacher was very nice, but she should have prepared different class tests for the two sections. We had discovered that the Cicero text to be translated into Italian she had chosen for one section was the same one she would then give to us, so very often we knew what test to expect! I loved Latin, and even when the teacher gave us tests that we had not seen before I always received excellent marks.

Orlando Furioso

The Science teacher had not managed to capture our attention, and the hour-long lesson was incredibly boring. I decided to do something interesting and started to write a poem parodying Orlando Furioso with our least-loved teachers as protagonists. Unfortunately, one day the teacher's eyes fixed on me, and I had to hand over my poem. I am still waiting for her to give it back to me; perhaps she liked it so much that she kept it for her own amusement.

Madre Moschino

At school my closest friends were Anna, Giovanna, Teodora and Assuntina. I spent time with them at school, and then in the afternoons, when we would get together to study, and to talk about our platonic loves. Very often I walked or cycled to Anna's house, sometimes Giovanna would come to study Philosophy with me, sometimes I went to Assuntina's house in the evening, but I rarely met up with Teodora because she lived in a different town.

We had made up names for each of the teachers who were nuns, and so the Italian teacher, a little nun with a hunched back who watched us with a sideways look became 'Madre Moschino' (which means 'little fly'); her real name was Clementina. This nun taught us Dante's Divine Comedy. When we got to the chapter where Dante speaks about Paolo Malatesta and Francesca da Rimini, the little nun told us we would be skipping those verses, and we immediately jumped to the page describing Paolo and Francesca's passionate love, while our teacher, with her nose stuck to the text, read on elsewhere.

A Bet

Anna and I had decided to bring some lunch to eat during the hour-long Philosophy class, betting that the teacher would not notice. We brought plates, cutlery and ham, eating this while our classmates laughed - the teacher did not notice a thing!

Playing Truant

One day I had the feeling that I would be interrogated in Chemistry the following day. This was another subject I hated, and I had to take measures ... what could I do? The only possibility was to stay at home, so I decided to play truant. I let Valeria in on the plan, and she decided to join me out of solidarity, certainly not because she needed to avoid the test too as she was very good at Chemistry. The following day we hid in the laundry room at the villa; I cannot remember whether we brought our school bags with us. We then headed down to the gate, and started walking towards Malpensa airport, but then had to turn around as we needed to be back by one. The next day I took a sick note to school which I signed myself – the note read "Absent due to illness".

Anna told me the teacher had called out my name. What a fright!

Strike For Trieste

That morning I remember that we students of the Magistrali heard the girls and boys of the Liceo Classico making a huge racket right under our windows: they were calling for us to join their strike, demonstrating against the occupation of Trieste.

We girls soon went down to join the Liceo boys and girls singing at the top of our voices through the streets of Gallarate 'Oh Trieste of my heart, we will come to free you'. We sang with such joy!

A Small Town In The Foothills Of The Alps

Re is a small town in the foothills of the Alps in Lombardy where we sometimes went for the weekend, staying in a cheap guesthouse. I remember the mountains in the distance, and the green meadows full of flowers where Valeria and I would lie in the sun. Mamma was always reluctant to leave our house, but when she was on holiday she never wanted to go back.

Canvasses And Paintbrushes

It was in one of those weekends in Re that I started to paint; lying on the grass I started transferring the landscape that surrounded me onto canvas. I remember that while I was painting, a boy came over to see the results on the canvas, and I felt like disappearing. I think I threw that painting away, but from that day I began one of my most intense activities, painting, using watercolours, oils, pastels and charcoal. I was 17 when I first picked up a paintbrush, and I continued to paint until nearly 2000 when I finished my last work 'Sunflowers'.

Young Maria Pia at work with her paintbrushes

A Guitar

Dear Papa! One evening he came home from Milan with a beautiful guitar for me, and I decided to take lessons along with a friend, but when she gave up I also stopped, abandoning the dream of being able to play the guitar one day. I always regretted not continuing with the lessons!

Papa often asked me to sing in front of the family, but I was so shy that even if it was just for family members I would have preferred to be swallowed up. I sang for Papa when he asked me to sing the song about the Piave, which no doubt reminded him of the years he spent on the front in the First World War.

My Youth & Adult Life

University

Once I had finished school, my great desire was to enrol at University to read Foreign Languages and Literature, and finally to learn English which I had not had the chance to do. I had always been fascinated by the English language; you could say I was in love with it. Learning English was my dream. Papa once again tried to impose his will on me, suggesting a career as a school inspector, but I hated the idea. Giovanna and Angelo were studying Economics and Engineering respectively, and I dreamt of University and the English language, but I knew that there was not much money for another of us, a daughter, to study. Papa suggested I could work doing sewing for an aunt who had a clothing business. I accepted the idea thinking I could have helped the family with my earnings, but I remember how sad I felt when I first sat down at the sewing machine. Fortunately, on that very day my finger ended up under the sewing machine needle resulting in an infection which ended my career in sewing.

I enrolled at Milan's Cattolica University in the Faculty of Foreign Languages and Literature.

Faculty Of Foreign Languages And Literature

I was so passionate about the English language that I suggested to my course mates to choose it as our main language, but they opted for Spanish; all it took was one meeting with the Professor of Spanish, an imposing woman who scared them by telling them not to expect an easy time just because Spanish resembles Italian. They came out with their tails between their legs and joined me in selecting English as their main language.

This is how my four-year course started in Milan: they were sometimes great, carefree times, but with the underlying fear that I would not be able to finish the course due to lack of money. In the meantime, Valeria had enrolled to study Mathematics before moving to the Faculty of Literature. Tonino later enrolled at Milan Polytechnic to study Engineering.

Milan

One of my happiest memories at Milan University was spending time with my friends; we would take the train at 6.55 in the morning. and return home in the evening, tired, laughing and chatting away. Mamma gave me 300 lire for lunch, and sometimes I ate at the canteen, but more often we went into the city centre, in Piazza Duomo, where near the Galleria Vittorio Emanuele there were two fantastic cafes, Alemagna and Motta; my friends and I went there to choose from the pastries, cakes and savoury delights. They were delicious! I realised that by going to one of the two cafés for lunch I could save nearly half the money Mamma had given me.

Sometimes we went for pizza at a fabulous Neapolitan pizzeria the name of which eludes me; I just know that it was in Via San Giovanni sul Muro. It was always full of students, and it was hard to find a space, not even a table, but a stool against a shelf on the wall.

I started teaching during my first year at University, helping primary school and later secondary school children. I remember that when I arrived home from University in the late afternoon I always found a group of children round the table for after-school lessons. One of these pupils was the son of the butcher where we went to buy meat, and I was so happy when I was paid by his parents because I could pay off the debt my family had with their shop.

A Dream Comes True

After I finished University, aware of the fact that I knew very little English, especially as we only had one hour of conversation with a mother tongue teacher, and he had to share his time among 80 students, I began thinking of deepening my knowledge of the language by going abroad for a period of time. My friends decided to go to London, where they enrolled in one of the many language schools. Fortunately, a cousin spoke to me about Dublin and, gripped by an irrepressible enthusiasm, I spoke to my family about the idea of going to Ireland. I had not counted on Papa, though, who immediately vetoed the plan, because he had read about two girls who had been killed in Dublin. Not even if a bomb had exploded in our house would there have been so much commotion; crying floods of tears seemed to get me nowhere until Mamma's sweet persuasion won Papa over, and I left.

I can still see the scene at Gallarate station in that far off July 1962: Mamma crying all her tears because maybe she felt that I would not come back to live in Italy. I embraced my family, and stepped onto the train with a friend whose name was Anna, beginning the long journey which would take us to Dublin.

Ireland

I arrived with my friend at Miss Wall's boarding house, 145 Tritonville Road, Sandymount, Dublin, with the intention of staying in Ireland for two months. I remained for nearly four years! As soon as I reached Ireland I realised I had not packed for the cold, damp climate. What to do? Anna said she had a great idea, and one evening we went into a pub, to the amazement of the men there, and she ordered a bottle of whisky, to even more astonishment on the faces of the customers! We went back to Miss Wall's, and in our room we began to sip the golden liquid; not being used to drinking, we felt so hot and red-faced that we fell asleep until the morning!

Not Even One Italian . . .

I had done all I could to avoid any Italians in Dublin as I was there to learn English, and certainly not to practice my Italian, so I was disappointed when one day I received an invitation to the Italian Embassy the following Sunday. I was doubly annoyed at the idea of wasting a lovely weekend afternoon, having to meet someone I knew nothing about.

Reliving the scene, I was led into a hall where this person, presumably the Italian Ambassador, was sitting at a desk: he then invited me to sit down in front of him. I asked myself what misdeeds I could have committed unknowingly, and then he opened his mouth and said candidly "How long has it been since you last wrote home, Doctor Genovesi?" Behind that question was the clear signature of Papa. I do not remember my exact reply, I think I said it had been two weeks, and we both burst out laughing.

What Good Fortune!

It was August, and the money I had brought with me was running out, but I wanted to stay longer in Dublin. I had been to the Italian Institute of Culture to ask if they needed a teacher, and they promised me something, but not until September.

Whether it was good fortune or divine intervention, while I was sitting in the sun in the Quadrangle one afternoon, three students came up to me and asked me if I was Italian, and I told them I was. They broke into big smiles, and asked me if I could help them prepare for their exams in autumn. I agreed without accepting any payment. They must have told the Professor of Italian about me because a few days later I received a call from the Italian Department of Trinity College asking me if I would like to teach.

A few weeks later I was contacted by the Department of Italian of Dublin's other University, UCD, proposing me the same. Furthermore, the Italian Institute of Culture offered me several teaching hours during the day and evenings, so I ended up being extremely busy. Every evening at 10 o'clock, after teaching my last class, I went to the Blue Lantern Cafe, off Grafton Street, and enjoyed omelette and chips and tea, reaching home before the stroke of midnight, exhausted but happy!

Papa finally stopped dreaming that his daughter would become a school inspector, and was over the moon to hear that I had become part of University life.

Elocution Lessons

I wished to speak English like an English person. I was fortunate enough to meet an elderly lady called Miss Ena Burke, living in Dawson Street, who ran an elocution school for actors and presenters wanting to perfect their pronunciation. I took ten half-hour lessons, and only stopped because Miss Burke told me I had learnt all there was to know.

The Most Important Meeting Of My Life

One day in September I was sitting at the dining room table listening to Radio Luxembourg, when the door opened and in walked Michael. Miss Wall introduced him to me. She had told me that a young English student was coming to stay, and that he was always smiling. I immediately noticed his fashionable short back and sides haircut and the long raincoat he was wearing.

Michael soon became my best friend, and we started going out together; we used to meet at the University canteen, but more often at the little "Buttery" where he listened to my news. Every Saturday we would go to the cinema in O'Connell Street, and each Sunday we asked each other round, cooking the same dish of steak, chips, fried onions, grilled tomato and mushrooms, always accompanied by bread and the delicious Irish butter. Whenever Michael cooked for me, he impressed me with a new page of an old newspaper, which served as our tablecloth. At the weekend we liked to take the coach to explore the outskirts of Dublin or get the bus to Dun Laoghaire, Blackrock or Malahide. We went to all the student parties and danced to the music of the Sixties.

Our friendship continued until Michael fell in love with me, but I wanted to remain just friends as there was another student, an American called Robert who was courting me, and I was thinking about him, but strangely I realised I could not be as free and spontaneous with Robert as I was with Michael.

Saturday night in O'Connell Street, Dublin

Glendalough

During the first term at Trinity, a group of students of various nationalities had formed, including Michael and me, Hans (Dutch), Marianne (Autrian), Tim (Irish) and Susan (English). Led by Hans we decided to explore the Irish countryside, and decided to go to Glendalough in County Wicklow. We set off from Dublin early on a Saturday morning with a coach that took us just outside the city, with the idea of walking the rest of the way. I remember vividly that after hours of walking we found ourselves in a bog, with our feet in the water, and we all turned to Hans who was holding the map. We burst out laughing, and I cannot remember exactly what happened until, absolutely exhausted, we reached the Glendalough youth hostel where I cooked spaghetti for everyone. That night, instead of staying with the rest of the group, I was fortunate to go to a B&B with Susan as there was not enough room at the hostel. The following morning, I discovered two great drawbacks of our accommodation: the toilet was a privy at the back, and I had unknowingly eaten black pudding for breakfast!

A few days ago, Michael asked me if I had noticed that he had made a big effort to sit next to me on the way back to Dublin.

Maria Pia in Glendalough, Ireland

Trinity College

In 1963 Trinity had become a daily meeting place for Michael and me at the "Buttery" where we met for lunch or the library, which was open until 10 o'clock at night. I like to cast my mind back to May evenings, when we left the library together while it was still light, crossed the Quadrangle, heading home.

Together with two other girls I knew, I organised a party one evening at my flat in Raglan Road, asking each of them to invite no more than ten people, but the word had got round at Trinity, and I ended up with a crowd of strangers.

Robert asked me to dance, but after a while we had to stop dancing because the music had ended abruptly. I thought it strange, but Michael later confessed that he had turned off the record player after getting annoyed watching Robert and me dancing to song after song!

In spring 1964 Michael and I flew to Exeter, touring Devon and Cornwall for a short holiday. It was then that Michael started talking about marriage. He told me recently that, at that time, I had looked at him in surprise, exclaiming "You have not asked me to marry you yet!"

Maria Pia & Michael at a party in Dublin

The Ambassador And Other Important People

I had already met the Italian Ambassador to Ireland. The Institute of Culture often invited Irish nobility, and that is how I had the opportunity of meeting President De Valera, an affable and charming man.

One day I was asked to go to the airport to meet the Nobel prize winner Salvatore Quasimodo, a Sicilian poet. I remember that when there was an evening in his honour I walked up to the poet, and told him how much I loved his simple and short poem "Everyone stands alone at the heart of the world, pierced by a ray of sunlight, and suddenly it is evening".

A Sad Evening

That evening of 22 November 1963 I went as usual to the Italian Institute of Culture to teach two classes of adults, but as soon as I got there the secretaries looked up sadly, and told me President Kennedy had been killed in Dallas that day. With a heavy heart I went up to the room where around forty adults were gathered in silence, and I simply said that I would not be able to teach them that evening as I was so shaken. J. F. Kennedy was for Irish people like a member of the family; I recall that during a trip to Wexford I had noted that a portrait of the Kennedy family was on display in all the windows, and I know that there would be a photograph of the Kennedys among family photos in many homes.

Caught In The Act

It was the night before the Christmas break, and Michael had taken me to the theatre; afterwards I invited him back to see where I was staying. He accepted my invitation, and we arrived at Trinity Hall a few minutes after nine p.m. As soon as we stepped into the room I was sharing with Margaret, an English student of mine, and Anne from America, the two girls shouted "Maria, don't you know that boys can't be here after half past eight!?" Michael walked over to the large window, but underneath there was a drop of several metres that made it impossible to escape, and so he decided to walk back down the long corridor to the exit. At around 11 o'clock Margaret told me that Michael was still in the lobby with Miss Darling, one of the two 'Generals' who ran the Hall of Residence; obviously the poor man had been stopped and interrogated.

Sometime later Michael gave me a full account of what had befallen him after he left the room. Here it is in his own words: 'Walking along the corridor I lost my sense of direction, realising that I must have made a wrong turn when I came across several girls in their night-dresses, who screamed when they saw me, and ran into their rooms, slamming their doors. After wandering around various corridors I eventually found myself in the entrance hall, but there was Miss Darling blocking the exit. By now it was getting quite late. "What are you doing wandering around at this time of night?" she exclaimed. I answered with the first thing I could think of "I was looking for the Gents". She was furious, exclaiming "There are no men's toilets here! Who were you with?" Not wanting to get Maria Pia into trouble I replied "I don't know her name, I only met her today." Miss Darling looked shocked, and she continued to question me. I refused to disclose the name and Miss Darling got more and more angry. Eventually I relented and said "I think her name may be Mary", and with that she summoned someone to wake up all the Marys in Trinity Hall, and got them to line up around the wall, in their nighties, and looking half asleep. Mary is a very common name in Ireland, and there must have been nearly 20 girls there. I was made to walk past the line with Miss Darling asking each one "Do you know this man?". Each one shook her head. It was midnight, and I was getting tired, so at Miss Darling's insistence I gave her my name; she unlocked the main door and let me go'.

The next day I saw Michael on the other side of the Trinity square, and he called out to me "I have to leave the University" making me almost faint, but immediately afterwards he said that he was joking. He then told me that he had been summoned to appear before the Junior Dean, who made him write an apology to Miss Darling, though he seemed to be amused at the whole episode.

The morning after our adventure, I was called into the office of Miss Bramble, the head, who was quite surprised that it was I that had been at the heart of the unrest, as she expected it had been Maria, the Spanish assistant, to have broken the rules.

.

Hitch-Hiking To Galway

I had been to Galway with my friend Anna in August 1962, just a month after our arrival, as Miss Wall had suggested we go to the famous races. We went by train and reached the races, but soon turned back because of the cold and classic Irish drizzle – we did not get to see a single horse!

This time it was different. Michael organised a weekend in Galway at the end of May; we set off from Dublin, and hitchhiked to the outskirts of Galway. From there we caught a bus which took us to just a few miles from Roundstone, our destination, but too far to reach on foot.

Michael was sure that someone would come along within a few minutes, and give a lift to two tired and hungry travellers. But no, we waited for ages until finally a tractor appeared and the farmer told us to jump onto the hay on the trailer, and started chatting with us, but the noise of the engine drowned him out, and we could not understand his accent anyway. Laughing our heads off, we arrived in Roundstone, a pearl on the Atlantic Ocean, with a stunning white sandy beach surrounded by fields of daisies.

Years later, during a nostalgic return trip to Ireland, we went back to Roundstone, but what a disappointment, the fields of daisies had been replaced by lines of caravans!

Maria Pia & Michael walking in Galway 1965

Maria Pia & Michael, Trinity College, Dublin

At the Races in Trinity College gardens, Dublin

Like A Queen

One morning, as soon as I arrived at the Italian Institute of Culture where I taught every morning and evening, the two secretaries cornered me, and asked me if I would represent the Institute at a ceremony organised by the Young Christian Democrats that was being held the following Sunday in a hotel. Seeing my obvious reluctance, they added that the German Institute would also be sending a representative; I was eventually persuaded to go. By then Michael and I were inseparable, and the pair of us got on a bus, heading towards the venue which was outside Dublin. It was then that we discovered that the hotel in question was in open countryside. I still do not know what inspired me to wear my little red cotton dress with black velvet collar and cuffs, rather than my usual weekend jeans. The shoes went with the dress, but were certainly not suitable for country walking, so right from the start I realised that something was not right, but let me describe that unforgettable evening.

Michael and I went into the lobby where we were greeted by the usher who led us to the hall where we sat down. It dawned on us that all the women were sitting on one side, and the men on the opposite one! Then we waited and waited for a good quarter of an hour until someone approached me, and asked me with a smile "By any chance would you be Dr Genovesi?" My mind was saying 'noooo', but I got up, wanting to disappear; my embarrassment increased because the usher asked me to follow him to the lobby. I had to make a grand entrance into the hall, to the applause of those present, and a bow from the nephew of the Provost of Trinity College. We were asked to sit at the high table, and the banquet began. I thought maybe I could eat in peace, but the nephew of the Provost then informed me that I was expected to make a speech! I was not sure if I had heard correctly, but he told me that everyone was waiting for me to speak. I turned to my angel of the moment, Michael, and asked him if he could stand up instead of me (at least he speaks English well, I thought), but I realised this would not do, so I begged the Provost's nephew to speak on my behalf, but he encouraged me. I stood up, my heart in my mouth, and managed to say something like "Good evening, I'm sorry I wasn't given any information about you, so I haven't prepared anything. I wish you all a great future"; then I sat down. I wondered what had happened to my German colleague, at the same time I decided that the following morning I would murder the two secretaries who had plunged me into this situation. I assumed the worst was over but no, because after the meal there was a dance. They asked me what music I liked to which I replied "Eine kleine nachtmusik". The Provost's nephew invited me to dance, while his girlfriend danced with Michael, I in my simple little dress, the nephew in a tuxedo and his girlfriend in an elegant long dress.

After the dance I started to understand something about the Young Christian Democrats because they projected in the hall a film of Kennedy's visit to Berlin. At the end, Michael and I wished our hosts goodbye; they presented me with an enormous bouquet of flowers. I said I didn't speak any Irish apart from "Cead mile failte", (which means "a thousand welcomes"). Great applause, and we were led to a taxi just outside the entrance. I waved from the window as the car moved off, just like a Queen!

As soon as we were out of sight, we started laughing our heads off until we reached Dublin.

The Good And The Bad

Among all the places I lived in Dublin the nicest was without a doubt Raglan Road, especially in spring when the cherry trees were blossoming. Would you like me to tell you about the worst place I stayed? Portobello Road! I shared one room with a family of fleas that I was unable to see as the old carpet was so dark, but I could feel them on my feet every time they jumped. The other irritation was caused by Rosemary Gibson, a lovely and eccentric student who every night would play and sing the then famous Blowin' in the wind on her guitar. A beautiful song, but sleep was impossible. The funny thing is that when she heard that I could not sleep all night she asked her father, a well-known insomnia therapist, to visit me, and he gave me a record with help for sleeping. However, as long as that guitar played, Bob Dylan was the soundtrack of my wakeful hours.

The First Term Of 1965

At the end of the first term of 1965, I said goodbye to Ireland where I had lived four happy and carefree years, where the Lord had called me to meet my soul mate. At the age of 17, I remember I had knelt by my bed and prayed "Lord, please help me meet someone who will love me my whole life long". My great friend in Ireland became my *Promesso Sposo*.

Giovanna from Verona took my place in Trinity; we became firm friends and we remain so to this day.

Having moved back to Italy I immediately started teaching in a number of schools, and began to prepare for 12 July 1966, the day Michael and I had set for our wedding.

The Two Generals

This is the nickname that Valeria and I had coined for Aunt Teresa and Aunt Angiolina, two of Papa's sisters. As if Papa's iron authority were not enough, they also had the task of protecting us from the world.

We started to go on holiday to the seaside in Marina di Massa, in Tuscany, where the aunts had a lovely villa. We were teenagers, and the first time we arrived there was a conflict between the aunts and Valeria, who was cheeky and rebellious. The aunts would not allow us to go and stroll on the promenade where people used to gather to admire and being admired. Valeria kept on pleading and the aunts wrote to Papa asking for his permission, which was denied. Valeria and I thought of bypassing any paternal authority, and made it possible for the aunts to be invited to a friend's nearby house to watch Television, while the two of us went secretly strolling on the sea front.

The most hilarious memory of our aunts Teresa and Angiolina involves Michael at the time we were engaged, when he came to Marina di Massa to visit me. Every night they locked the door of the room where he slept imagining what ardent passion might have exploded in the night, so poor Michael had to jump from the window into the garden every time he needed a pee! Fortunately, the window was only a metre or so high.

12 July 1966

The most important day of my life, a day with just a bit of melodrama.

That morning Mamma came to wake me, I had been awake for much of the night and had only fallen asleep when it was nearly morning. I was anxious about the walk from the big doors of Saint Mary's Basilica to the altar because I was afraid of fainting in front of everyone, and it would not have been the first time. Having reached the spot where Michael was waiting for me, we walked together towards the Monsignor, telling him I had drunk a sip of whisky to steady my nerves. Michael knew of my fear so had come prepared, and throughout the ceremony he kept offering me sugar lumps or smelling salts. Thankfully, I did not need the salts or sugar, which he had in his jacket pocket. Nobody would have noticed the melodrama had the Monsignor not declared at the end of the ceremony "the bride did not faint!".

Maria Pia & Michael at the Wedding Reception at Villa Aminta, Stresa, Italy

My Little Bride

The first place we lived in as a married couple was the single room Michael rented in Victoria, near Imperial College, where he was studying for a PhD in Physics.

The first few evenings of our life together we went to eat in a trattoria where we only ordered spaghetti al pomodoro as we could not spend more, but fortunately the waiter also brought us some bread. Michael then said that we could not afford to eat out, so I started cooking in our little room; every evening I would surprise him with a meal which I cooked on an electric hotplate.

We were very happy, I was deeply in love with Michael, who called me "my little bride".

There are some memories that add colour, though not always pleasant; in this case it was the crazy woman living in the room next door to us, who did not want me to use the shared wash basin to clean my teeth.

A Hovel

After a few weeks in our first nest Michael began to look for another place for us. As we had no income apart from his student grant, there was only one miserable choice available to us, a cramped one-bedroom flat. The unscrupulous landlord had never thought about doing anything to make that hovel inhabitable: the sofa sagged to the ground, the curtains were ragged and black with smog, the bathroom was always freezing because there was only a tiny heater attached to the ceiling, and layer upon layer of dirt and grease from previous tenants had built up all around the cooker. Every morning I would be down on my knees trying in vain to clean up that grease.

Down To Earth With A Bump

It became clear that I needed to find a job, but my degree was not recognised in the UK; fortunately, one day I saw an advertisement for nursery staff, and I raced over. I have always liked children, and I was already thinking about a job looking after them, but how disappointed was I when the two staff members told me I would only be cleaning. The two, one English the other Australian, greeted me by saying "We are very proud of being British citizens". I could not face writing home to tell my family about my sad situation. Every morning those two arrogant women instructed me to wash the window frames and the steps of the nursery; when I mentioned that I had already done it the previous day they ordered me to do it again. The whole time I was working as a servant I could hear the children shouting in a big room upstairs; there was no teaching happening, though the advertisement had mentioned Montessori, Froebel and other methods.

I put up with the situation and carried on for a few weeks, but I felt a sense of shame whenever I saw a mum or dad collect their little ones in the evening, so one day I decided to act. I called the number on the advertisement and let the owner of the nursery know how things were being run. She begged me to stay on, but I turned her down. Better off poor than being part of that fraud.

A Christmas Parcel

When we moved to that squalid little flat in Alperton one of the highlights of the Christmas holidays was receiving a parcel from Mamma. She used to send a box full of Italian patisserie treats. It was a great joy to open it and discover its contents with cries of delight. I would, however, delay opening the Christmas parcel for a day as I wanted to make the enjoyment last a little longer.

I did the same with the letters from Michael when I was alone in Dublin and he was in Ipswich, and with letters from home in Italy when we lived in England.

Hard Times

Michael's grant for his PhD was only £10 a week, but over £7 went on rent, so we found it difficult to make ends meet. Fortunately, there was a lack of primary school teachers at that time, and I found out that, as a secondary school teacher, I could do a special training course to be able to teach primary classes. I was chosen as a teaching assistant in a primary school in London, and it was a beautiful period: the children loved me and I loved them. In the morning I helped Mairi, a lovely Scottish lady who soon became my dear friend, but in the afternoon I had the whole class of 42 six-year-olds. I left the school at the end of the first term as I was pregnant: a joy was on its way!

Mariella Arrives

We lived in the upper floor flat of a terraced house on the North Circular Road, squeezed between a cemetery and the Piccadilly Line. To our joy Mariella was born, and I was no longer alone during the day; Mariella was my little companion and filled my day. Every morning I took her in the pram to the only green space nearby, and then carry on to the shops, sometimes walking an extra half a mile to buy carrots which cost a halfpenny less.

More Difficult Times

They were hard times, but we were happy. Michael started mending radios and televisions in the evenings to earn some extra money, and would sometimes work into the small hours. I cannot tell you how disappointed he was when he was unable to mend something.

I found it hard to adapt, and could not fall asleep until he came to bed. The days went by fast. I remember that a few days before Christmas, when I was six months pregnant, we received a tax rebate, enough to buy two plane tickets to fly to Italy and spend Christmas with my family. We were only able to go for four days. What a joy!

Our Other Great Joy

To make me happy, Michael accepted a research position at Milan Polytechnic with a two-year contract. We rented a flat in Gallarate, the town where I was born and where I grew up. It was so lovely to see my dear family in Italy, and to be able to speak to them in person instead of just over the phone. It was expensive for us to call Italy, and when I phoned on special occasions such as birthdays, I ended up barely being able to say "Ciao" before having to hang up. Our little Mariella quickly adapted to the new routine; I was so happy whenever I was out with her in the pushchair, and I bumped into Mamma in town, usually at the fruit and vegetable market. She would often take us to Pasticceria Bianchi, famous for its patisserie.

That spring Anthony arrived, the other great joy of our lives, but after the birth I ended up in a coma, and was saved by a young doctor whose name I still remember – Dr Avanzini. When I finally left the hospital and was able to go back home, I found myself with two young children to look after. I soon met Licia, a lovely lady who lived in the same apartment block with her husband and her little boy Max; we became great friends. I started having bad headaches, and Licia used to come down to get Anthony who was just a few months old, and looked after him for the whole day. Licia and I used to take Max and Mariella to the kindergarten every morning, and she often invited me and Anthony to eat with her.

We lived not far from my sister Valeria, so Mariella had two play-friends in cousins Rocco and Luca. Michael returned home tired in the evening but we were happy.

Maria Pia & Michael with little Anthony

We Leave Italy

Lovely things do not always last, the most beautiful roses have thorns. After two years Michael's contract ended, and he found himself out of a job. He answered an advertisement in Nature magazine for a research physicist specialised in Photoelectronics at University College London. He was invited to an interview in London despite the deadline having already passed. Michael flew to London, and that same evening he called me to say "They want me, what shall I do?" With a broken heart I told him to accept, and that is what he did. The day we were leaving, Mamma surprised me by coming round at seven in the morning saying "This day had to come, Pia!" She had crossed the entire town on foot!

Seven Years In Feering

We found a house in Feering in Essex, and Michael started working at University College London, coming back late in the evening, his train very often delayed by signal failure. I was so homesick for Italy, and imagined seeing Mount Rosa when I looked out of the kitchen window. Anthony was only 14 months old, and Mariella, who was four, started at the village school the following school year, but did not get on with the noisy atmosphere, so we moved her to a convent school in a more tranquil location.

Oxfordshire

At UCL Michael led a small group preparing part of the IUE (International Ultraviolet Explorer) satellite for NASA. After seven years, when the project was completed, he was transferred to Rutherford Laboratory, near Oxford, where he worked on the IRAS satellite project surveying the sky for infrared sources. We moved to Abingdon, a pretty little town on the banks of the Thames, where we live to this day. I remember that every morning I took Anthony, who was then seven, to a family who drove a small group of children to the European School, while Mariella went to the School of St Helen and St Katharine.

I recall the days when our two jewels left home to go to University: Mariella went to Oxford, Anthony chose Edinburgh, such a long way away from us. The first day they left home I said to myself, forlornly "Tonight they are not sleeping here!" I thought of Mamma's sorrow, when I left Italy.

Club Italia

When we came to live in Abingdon, I got a job teaching Italian as a foreign language at the European School; at the same time, I was offered a position teaching Italian at the Abingdon College of Further Education, where I taught for many years. The loveliest time was when I started an Italian conversation class at our home. One evening a week, under my guidance, seven adults would gather in our lounge to speak in Italian, and the number soon doubled. The atmosphere was so nice, and they were all so clearly happy to be here. On the rare occasions when I was not well, Anthony took my class, and I would hear my students' laughter as they enjoyed Anthony's antics. I remember one evening when Mariella decided to stand outside the living room window in full view of the class – she was wearing my wedding dress! You can imagine how everyone laughed!

Many of my students have become my friends, including Cristina, Melanie, Colin and Carol.

. . . . and Other Animals

Gerald Durrell's book "My family and other animals" has amused many who have read it, and thinking about it there have been other animals in our family as well.

In the villa where I was born there was Lea who was our guard dog, and after her came Loris, her son. Angelo, who loved hunting, brought home a beautiful pointer, Kali who very soon demonstrated that he was not cut out for hunting, as he ran home with his tail between his legs whenever he heard a shot.

And then there were the hens, many hens.

When we lived in Feering the children were small, and to bring them joy we bought a hamster, which they named Beppe, who was adventurous enough to climb up behind the piano, and then jump down on the carpet. Hamsters are nocturnal, and you never know what they do at night. After him came Beppe 2, and then Beppe 3, followed by Pippa 1, after which we decided to interrupt the dynasty as our garden was becoming too full of little graves.

One morning I found one of these animals looking very poorly, and I gave him an extra lease of life by putting him in the airing cupboard, administering drops of whisky!

After we came to live in Abingdon the animal kingdom expanded with the arrival of two lovely bunnies, Thumper for Anthony and Fudge for Mariella. Later uncle Tonino, who had come to visit us, gave us two budgies, Bianca for Mariella and Gregory for Anthony. No, this was not enough, because both Mariella and Anthony began dreaming of having a dog, and they pleaded so much that one day I agreed, and together we went to choose a Golden Retriever puppy. Michael was in America at the time, and returning one night he found a live bundle of fur in the kitchen! We all agreed on a name for the new arrival: Tess, but since she was a pedigree Golden Retriever, we learned that her full name was Tess Dearflight Midnight Minuet! With this name we thought she would have a little more intelligence, but we were immediately disappointed; Mariella and Anthony took her to an obedience class. Tess returned home without having learnt anything.

The kingdom of invertebrates was also represented in our home zoo, and in fact Mariella was the keeper of two stick insects to which she had given the names Cromwell and Cleopatra.

Mariella & Tess

84

Healed!

It was just a few days before Christmas 1990, but no preparations had been made, no joy in the house, because I was ill. I had been in bed for 15 days due to what was later diagnosed as intoxication from the migraine medication I had been prescribed. The headaches were getting worse, to the point that at 11 at night they were turning into a monster. Michael could not even talk to me because I was unable to speak. He phoned the surgery to explain the situation, but was told that hospital patients were given much bigger doses than I was on.

Michael managed to get an appointment, via our GP, at the Neurology Department of the John Radcliffe Hospital in Oxford, and we took a taxi as I could not stand up. When we got there, we were told that the clinic was closed. I was made to lie down under an enormous bright light, I have no idea why, and after a while I was told to go into a room where someone would see me. Alone in the room Michael began to say "Oh Pia, I'm so sorry, I thought I was taking you to the best possible place", but I interrupted him saying "Don't worry, I believe in Jesus!". At that very moment the door opened, and a young Registrar, Dr Michael Donoghue, walked in; after speaking to me he immediately realised I was being poisoned by my medication.

I will always remember Dr Michael Donoghue who saved me! Later I found out that he had given up his lunch break to see me! The medicine he gave me freed me from all the toxins, and two days later Mariella and Anthony came home from university to celebrate Christmas together!

Abigail

To the great joy of all the family, our first grand-daughter was born - Abigail Katie, Mariella and Marco's first daughter. That very evening we were faced with the worst crisis our family has ever endured. It began with Abigail not being able to feed during her first day of life. The situation continued that night and the next day, but the midwife on duty did not realise that Abigail was in fact suffering from peritonitis. So, on that second night, Mariella was given a sleeping tablet to let her have some respite following two sleepless nights. Our daughter was woken up abruptly by the hospital staff, who told her to hurry to her baby who was very ill. Mariella, still under the effects of the sleeping tablet, saw Abigail, who was already in toxic shock, and phoned Marco to ask him to come straight away. There were no facilities for treating Abigail at Bedford hospital so she was stabilised before being taken the two hours' journey by ambulance to Leicester Royal Infirmary. That night our son-in-law Marco phoned us to ask us to pray, because he and Mariella were following the ambulance which was carrying their baby girl, not knowing whether they would find her alive in Leicester. I remember praying "Jesus, please, don't take Abigail!" I immediately felt the Lord saying to me "Be still and know that I am God" which is in Psalm 46, my favourite Psalm now. Michael and I travelled to Leicester to see our little grand-daughter, who had been placed in ICU; I had never seen such a tiny body with so many tubes attached. After two months in hospital Abigail, was finally able to return home shortly before Christmas - a miracle!

In The Holy Land

In October 2014, to celebrate our Golden Wedding Anniversary, we went on a pilgrimage to the Holy Land, something I had wanted to do for many years. We thus had the chance to walk in the footsteps of Jesus, in Cana, Galilee, where He had turned water into wine, and there we renewed our vows.

Having a personal relationship with Jesus made us fall in love even more than before, so much so that we sometimes dance in the kitchen to the music of the Sixties as if we were still in our twenties.

Tiberias

The visit to the Holy Land started on the Mount of Olives, where Jesus wept over Jerusalem, but for the two of us it ended unexpectedly in Tiberias on the Sea of Galilee. This is where the miraculous catch of fish had taken place after Jesus had asked Peter to cast the net in the water one more time; they brought a huge number of fish to the shore, to the amazement of the disciples who had been fishing all night without catching anything.

The day before we were due to fly home I came down with severe bronchitis. In the morning we had been with the group on a boat similar to that used in the time of Jesus, for the typical sea trip, after which the programme included a visit to Capernaum. While we were on the way to this site, I started to feel unwell; the heat was oppressive and my head was spinning, so I was unable to explore the place with the other pilgrims. Instead, I sat on a wall in the shade to wait for the rest of the group to return from visiting the ruins of the temple and Peter's house, which are there in Capernaum. We then all returned to the coach, which took us to a restaurant to enjoy the so called "Peter's fish". They had prepared a large table laden with the local produce, including, naturally, Peter's fish. I could not bring myself to even look at the plate in front of me; Michael called a taxi which took the two of us back to the hotel, and I went straight to bed with a temperature of 39 C. Within the space of half an hour I started to cough so violently that I found it hard to breath.

There was a young doctor in our group, and she came up to the room to see me telling me the fever would get worse during the night, and I ought to go to a clinic in the morning. I was unable to sleep because of the wheezing sounds coming from my lungs and I started to panic; I gripped the medal of Jesus the Nazarene that I always wear round my neck, and prayed "Jesus, I am afraid, help me!" Towards four in the morning, I woke up completely free of the cough, with no fever, and feeling completely calm. I drank lots of grapefruit juice that the hotel had provided for me and rested till morning. The hotel allowed us to stay in our room until a taxi came to take us to Tel Aviv airport, where we met up with our group for the flight home that evening. Throughout the entire flight I felt completely well, but once home the bronchitis returned and continued its course for a few days. Jesus had made it possible for me to return home without difficulty. I realised afterwards that if my cough and fever had not subsided the authorities would not have allowed me to fly. What a blessing!

On the Sea of Galilee

The Call of Italy

The call of Italy was always strong: every year we travelled to Italy to spend Christmas with *i nonni*, choosing Mamma's birthday on December 20 as the day to arrive in Gallarate, where we stayed with Valeria and Pietro and their sons Rocco and Luca.

Every summer we went to Marina di Massa, a lovely seaside town in Tuscany where Valeria joined us with her little ones.

When Mamma became gravely ill, I travelled to Italy to help my sisters Giovanna and Valeria look after her. I stayed a month in Italy, and before my return I asked Michael to prepare two extra beds as I would be bringing Rocco and Luca home with me, in order to give Valeria the chance to look after Mamma.

It was early January 1978. We had just come back from Gallarate, where we had spent a lovely Christmas with the family, when we received a call from Valeria telling us that Mamma's health had deteriorated and she would not last long. Michael had to leave later that day for a work trip to the NASA laboratory in Pasadena, USA; he managed to buy three plane tickets for me and the children before he left. We landed at Malpensa airport in a snow storm. Mariella and Anthony found themselves living with their cousins once more, and joined their primary school.

Even though we knew that these were Mamma's last months, I felt at peace, and I was able to be near, and sometimes read her some prayers. She called me "Speranza", which means "Hope".

Mamma passed away on April 6th of that year.

Little Mariella wrote this line dedicated to nonna Carmen "Heaven's love is the biggest in the world and the angels will love you forever".

Grandchildren

We have six fantastic grandchildren, ranging in age from five to 25.

Alessio was born in 1995. That day I remember a tiny goldcrest flew onto our rose 'Peace'. Alessio is very reserved, loving nothing more than cosying up with the family to watch a film. He likes television - when he was five or six, while visiting the ruins of a medieval castle with his family, he stepped into what was once a room, and exclaimed "This must be where they watched their videos!"

Luca was born in 1998. He is very creative and loves writing, including poetry. He is highly talented musically; when I ask him what he is playing on the piano he says he is just improvising. He is also talented on the guitar, which he taught himself to play.

Abigail was born in 2000, and two days later we nearly lost her as is recounted in the chapter dedicated to her. With a joyful nature and an irrepressible faith, she is passionate about evangelising. She has that rare gift of empathy, which enables her to help those around her.

Eleanor was born in 2003. When she was little, I used to call her by the Italian version of her name, Eleonora, and when I did, she turned to me with eyes full of laughter and the smile of a diva. We gave her a piano a while ago to encourage her with her musical talent, and when she visits us she always delights us with her playing.

William was born in 2008. He has had a love of adventure since his earliest years. One morning when he was two years old, he managed to open the front door and run out . . . but let me describe the scene: Anthony, his daddy, was already at work, but luckily his mummy heard the door open – with her heart in her mouth she ran outside and saw William running down the pavement dressed just in a nappy, wellington boots and a pair of sunglasses! His plan was to cross the very busy A10 to go and buy an ice-cream!

Greta was born in 2015. From a very early age, Greta showed she had an ear for music, trying to dance before she could even walk. She loves nature and enjoys going for long walks in the woods with Anthony, stopping to pick flowers for the table. She loves all animals, even worms, and recently built a grave for a worm which had fallen from a bird's beak, decorating the "worm heaven" with leaves and twigs.

Acknowledge Me . . . Luke 12:8

Mamma taught us from when we were little (there were five of us) never to ignore a hand stretched out to us, and I dare say I have always had a soft spot for the homeless in my heart, so I am not surprised that wherever I go I can be sure to meet Jesus. At the beginning of each journey, whether it is to Oxford or just Abingdon, I send up a simple prayer: "Where do You want me to put down the nets today?"

I met Steve and Oscar (Oscar is Steve's handsome black Labrador) many years ago, about 2002, outside Marks & Spencer. It was my first encounter with a complete stranger to whom I wanted to mention the Saviour; so I sent a quick prayer on the Royal telephone "Jesus, help!" I am so shy but all shyness went when I stopped in front of the dog. Words came out of my mouth, and I started to say something like "Oh, what a lovely dog, what's his name?" "Oscar" "And yours?" "Steve" "Pleased to meet you, Steve. May I buy a sandwich for you?" "Oh, yes, please". After putting a delicious looking sandwich and a bottle of lemonade in his hand I added "Steve, do you know about Jesus? He loves you". Steve smiled and showed me a necklace to which were attached a few holy medals.

I carry in my pocket some small strips of paper with promises from the Bible, so I gave one of these to Steve, and I left him saying "I will pray for you, Steve. I'll pray that you will find a roof over your head, a home that you can share with Oscar". Two weeks later I found myself in Oxford, this time with Michael, and by chance we met Steve, who was radiant because he had been allocated a place to live with his beloved Oscar! For years he had been applying for a room, but this had always been denied because of the dog. Much later we learned that Steve had been given a job in the Big Issue office in Oxford.

Years ago, in Oxford. Christmas time, people were passing by, intent on their own business and no one acknowledged this handsome young man playing the bagpipes (Oh, he so reminded me of our son Anthony when he was struggling to find a job in Edinburgh!). As I moved towards him, I saw that between him and me there was just one shop; I felt I needed more support from Above, so I entered this shop, went into a corner and just said "Lord, everyone is passing by this brother without even looking at him, I must tell him You love him, but he's playing now, what shall I do?" I went out, and walked towards the young man, who finished the tune just before I stopped in front of him. Then followed "Hello, what lovely music, where are you from?" "Australia" "What is your name?" "Heath" "Heath, Jesus loves you!" His face broke into a lovely smile when I mentioned the Name of Jesus.

What about Shane (in the photo with me)? I passed him by, but from the corner of my eye I spotted the Big Issue. I turned back, and before I reached him, he smiled and spoke to me "How are you today?" (He reminded me of Jesus, sitting at Jacob's Well, asking "Give me a drink"). "I'm fine, thanks" I replied "What's your name?" "Shane". After a while, on leaving him, I added "I will pray for you, Shane". "And I will for you" he answered.

Many, many more stories, many, many faces but in them I just see His face, the face of my Lord. I believe that the Lord has given me this mission also to heal a certain page of my life, when I was a little girl of six or seven. Almost every day the gate bell of the villa would ring, and I do not know why it was always I who ran down the steps to put a plain bread roll in the outstretched hand. I still remember the reluctance and frustration, because I knew that at the villa opposite ours it was not just a roll but a thick sandwich. Sometimes I could not make myself look at the beggar, I felt so sad. My sister Valeria and I often recalled this little story: we ran after a certain beggar who seemed different from all the others in posture and countenance, but we could not find him anywhere, so we liked to believe it could have been Jesus . . .

Before Covid Michael and I, together with our friends Maeve, Thérèse, Simon, Fr Phil, Richard and Carole, used to go regularly to find the homeless in the streets of Oxford. I asked the names of those we met, and then put them on a list; whenever I go to Communion, I take this list with me, and receiving Jesus, I hand them over to Him, for I do not know a better place.

Perhaps, when I finally go Home, I will see all these friends, and who knows, even Oscar!

With a homeless man in Oxford

The Little Shop Of Happiness

When Mariella and Anthony were small, I kept a journal which I called "The little shop of happiness". I recorded details of their daily life in it, their first words, their discoveries, their adventures and dreams. I started it in 1968 after Mariella was born and it spans all the years until our two jewels left for University.

Many Nice Things

I love walking in a wood and feel the divine silence around me, now and then interrupted by the birds singing in the trees, by the rustling of the leaves moved by the wind, by the murmur of a brook, and I wish that my walking could go on for ever.

I like turning my eyes to the starry sky when everything is quiet, and then I look for the constellations I know, and the stars of which I know the names. I recall one evening when Michael and I were on the Isle of Elba; it was pitch dark, and we were walking on the sand towards a terrace where people were dancing. The starry sky seemed to touch the earth, and we were wrapped in a velvety mantle.

I love bird watching programmes, especially when they show the tiniest creatures like a gold crest or a tree creeper. Michael is used to my joyful exclamations at the sight of one of these little ones making a nest in our nesting box, or when they appear outside our bedroom window.

Gardening is one of my favourite occupations, and I spend hours tending to our flowers, plants and lettuces. I love preparing pots and baskets in the spring. We have 30 roses of different colours, and my favourites are Munstead Wood, Margaret Merril, and The Shepherdess.

Music enchants me, and often the Lord speaks to me through music, whether it is Opera, or popular songs. When Mariella and Anthony were teenagers, we treated them to Opera, Ballet, or Theatre as Christmas presents.

When I started teaching at the Abingdon College of Further Education, I found out that not far away there was a large hall, where every Monday evening someone was teaching Scottish Country Dancing, so one evening I went to see what it was all about. I instantly fell in love with the music and the elegant dances. I soon became an expert, and went to nearly every ball in our area. I was so taken by the music of Scottish dancing! One day we were in Edinburgh with Anthony and family. While we were walking near a place called The Mound I stopped at once as someone was playing a well-known tune. I could not resist the impulse that made me take off my shoes, and barefoot I danced across the whole square, and then came back to where Michael, Anthony and Katie were holding their breath. Even little William was looking at me in amazement amongst the cheering crowd!

My best television programmes are those about gardening, and documentaries about nature, with my favourite one being "Gardener's World".

I love cooking, and it is always a joy when I prepare various savoury dishes and desserts for family and friends, and see them enjoying the food. It is always a success, but not everyone knows that I have a 'Super Chef', Jesus of Nazareth who cooked fish on the beach for his disciples, and who always cooks with me!

The Avenue Of Linden Trees

The avenue of linden trees was the loveliest road in the town where I was born, very wide and flanked by these magnificent trees. In late summer they would be covered in garlands of intensely scented flowers which are used to make herbal teas.

Imagine my surprise one day when I was walking in our local park. I saw two linden trees, and walking underneath them the strong perfume from their flowers took me back to my childhood! I have another memory linked to the linden tree avenue: it continued up an incline around a hill, at the top of which is a tiny church where I was baptised.

A Journey Of Faith

From childhood I have always known about God: I was afraid of God the Father, I did not know God the Son, and I did not know what God the Holy Spirit was. Nevertheless, I followed my parents to Mass every Sunday and every morning during the month of May. It was lovely to walk up the hill to Midnight Mass as a family. What a joy it was on the way back home when snowflakes were falling.

During the Christmas season Mamma would gather us little ones around the crib every evening to recite a beautiful poem "O cieli immensi", written by her teacher, a nun; I have taught it to Michael and to our children, and we still recite it today!

I had several spiritual experiences. On a certain Good Friday, for instance, as I was in the church of San Francesco in Gallarate with Mamma and Valeria, I wept thinking of Jesus on the Cross. However, I would have to wait many years before coming to know Jesus in my heart, and not just in my mind. It happened at the end of a spiritual journey, a course on the Baptism in the Holy Spirit, Whom I received when two believers prayed over me. I did not feel at all different at the time, but later, when I went to Mass and heard the Gospel proclaimed from the pulpit, I remember saying to myself "Oh, the Word is alive, Jesus is alive!" It was as if in that moment I passed from B.C to A.D – from before Christ to the year of our Lord! From that day I no longer felt that going to church was a burden, but simply a delight.

I remember as a little girl that every morning Mamma came into the room I shared with Valeria, and woke us with her sweet voice, saying "Get up, sing and work, the sun is here, and so is Mamma!" These words made such an impression that I did the same with our children.

Every evening Mamma ended her day with the words spoken by the two disciples on the road to Emmaus when they recognised Jesus "Abide with us Lord, for it is toward evening, and the day is almost over!" I too end my day with the same words "Abide with us!"

Epilogue

I am grateful to the Lord who allows us to enjoy the simple but priceless delight that the family brings, especially when Mariella with Marco come to visit us, with their magnificent Alessio, Luca, Abigail and Eleanor, and when Anthony and Katie come with their magnificent William and little Greta, filling the house with joy. When we are not busy with the family it is a privilege to be able to work in the vineyard of the Lord, dedicating ourselves to the homeless and to all those who need a listening ear. More and more institutes, schools, hospitals and other public buildings have closed the door to Jesus, and yet the world urgently needs Him, the Prince of Peace. My great desire is to be able to say to everyone "Jesus loves you, do not be afraid!"

<u>Appendix</u>

Some of Maria Pia's paintings.

Half Past Eleven
Oil on canvas
This painting was accepted by the Royal Academy for the 1985 Summer Exhibition

Girl with a Sun Hat
Watercolour

Alberobello
Oil on Canvas

Briar Rose
Watercolour

Stepping Out
Oil on canvas

Venice in the Mist
Watercolour

Sicilian Dance
Pastel

Watering Can
Oil on canvas

Sunflowers
Oil on canvas

Printed in Great Britain
by Amazon

17030181R00073